A practic

introduction to

Sage Line 50

Other Titles of Interest

A practical introduction to

Sage Line 50

David Weale

Bernard Babani (Publishing) Ltd
The Grampians
Shepherds Bush Road
London W6 7NF
England

Please Note

Although every care has been taken with the production of this book to ensure that any instructions or any of the other contents operate in a correct and safe manner, the Author and the Publishers do not accept any responsibility for any failure, damage or loss caused by following the said contents. The Author and Publisher do not take any responsibility for errors or omissions.

The Author and Publisher make no warranty or representation, either express or implied, with respect to the contents of this book, its quality, merchantability or fitness for a particular purpose.

The Author and Publisher will not be liable to the purchaser or to any other person or legal entity with respect to any liability, loss or damage (whether direct, indirect, special, incidental or consequential) caused or alleged to be caused directly or indirectly by this book.

The book is sold as is, without any warranty of any kind, either expressed or implied, respecting the contents, including but not limited to implied warranties regarding the book's quality, performance, correctness or fitness for any particular purpose.

No part of this book may be reproduced or copied by any means whatever without written permission of the publisher.

© 1999 BERNARD BABANI (publishing) LTD

First Published - September 1999

British Library Cataloguing in Publication Data

A catalogue record for this book is available from the British Library

ISBN 0 85934 480 0

Cover Design by Gregor Arthur

Cover Illustration by Adam Willis

Printed and bound in Great Britain by Bath Press

Preface

Welcome, I wrote this book to help you in learning how to use the program in a practical way. It is intended to explain the program in a way that I hope you will find useful, and that you will learn by doing.

Each section of the book covers a different aspect of the program and contains various hints and tips which I have found useful and may enhance your work. By working through the material and practising it, you will build up an expertise in the use of the applications.

The text is written both for the new user and for the more experienced person who wants an easy to follow reference. Please note that you should know how to use the basic techniques of Microsoft® Windows® 95/98; if you do not, there are many excellent texts on the subject.

I hope you learn from this book and have fun doing so.

David Weale, September 1999

Trademarks

Microsoft® and Windows® are registered trademarks of Microsoft® Corporation.

All other trademarks are the registered and legally protected trademarks of the companies who make the products. There is no intent to use the trademarks generally and readers should investigate ownership of a trademark before using it for any purpose.

About the author

David Weale is a Fellow of the Institute of Chartered Accountants and has worked in both private and public practice. At present, he is a lecturer in business computing.

Dedication

This is for my father, without whose guidance this particular book would never had been written.

Contents

The Tutorial

Preliminary tasks

Before you can begin the exercises, you need to carry out certain tasks.

Rebuilding (clearing) the data

Initially, you need to clear all the previous data (**after backing it up if necessary**) by pulling down the **File** menu and selecting **Maintenance**.

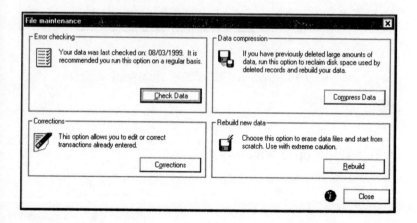

Click the **Rebuild** button.

Make sure all the ticks are removed from the boxes and this will rebuild your data files and clear all the existing data.

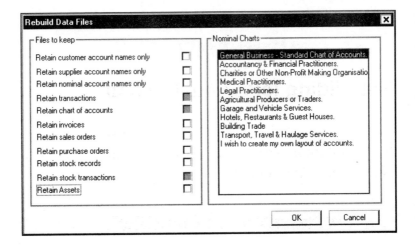

Next you will be prompted for the financial year, set it to **January 1999**

Close all the open windows.

The Financial Year (dates)

To check this, pull down the **Settings** menu and select **Financial Year**, you should see the dialog box shown below; alter the date to that shown (if necessary).

You cannot alter the date once you have begun to enter transactions into the program.

You should also make sure that the company name has been altered by pulling down the **Settings** menu, choosing **Company Preferences**, followed by **Address**.

Alter the details as shown below (this is important as this data will appear on reports and so on).

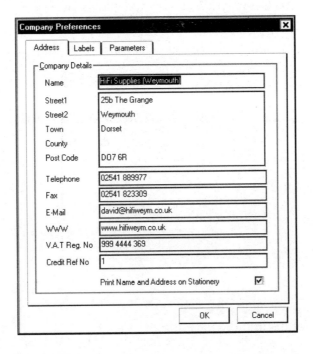

The Initial Screen

When you load Sage Line 50, you will see the main screen.

This contains the module buttons and the pull-down menus.

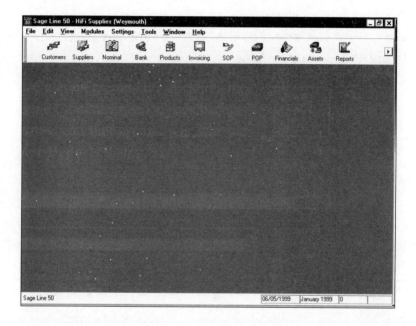

Note the arrow button on the right; clicking this enables you to see the other available buttons.

Sales Ledger

The Sales Ledger (called **Customers** within Sage) is used to record (credit) sales made to customers.

A credit sale is when the goods or services are supplied and an invoice is sent to the customer for payment later (normally within a month).

The basic data entered into the Sales Ledger is:

❖ Customers Names, Addresses and other necessary details.

❖ Details of the invoices sent to customers for goods or services supplied.

Each customer is allocated a separate account (sometimes more than one, for example, if there are different branches) and each account is given its own account code.

Entering Data into the Sales Ledger

After clicking the (left-hand) mouse button on **Customers** in the main Sage screen, you will see the **Customers** screen.

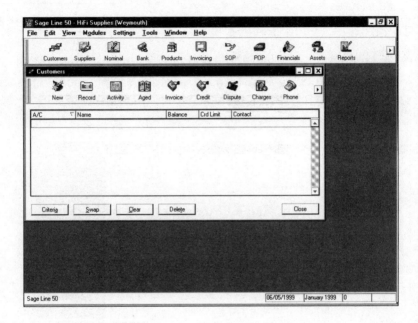

Recording Customer Details

The first task within the **Customers** module is to enter customer details (you cannot enter any other data until the customer details have been entered and saved).

To do so, click the **Record** button and the following screen will appear.

Record

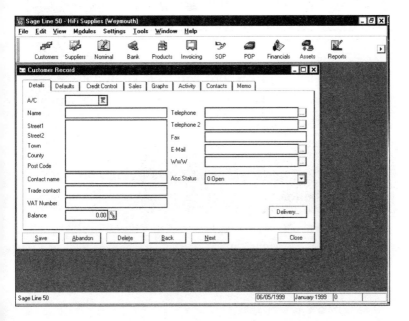

See how the screen is divided into fields, e.g. Name, Street1, etc., (each field contains a specific type of data in a similar way to a database).

You enter each customer's details within this screen.

If you do not want to enter data into a particular field use the **TAB** key to move to the next field (or click the mouse pointer within the next field).

You **must** save each record before moving onto the next; this is done by clicking on the **Save** button along the bottom of the screen.

If you make a mess and want to start again just click the **Abandon** button.

When you have finished entering both customers, click on the Close button and return to the Customers screen.

You are going to enter two customers; the data you need to enter is shown on the next page.

Customer Data to be entered

A/C	ADAMS	CANDY
Name	Adams Electrical	HiFi Store
Street1	33	Hilltops
Street2	High Street	New Road
Town	Somerton	Taunton
County	Somerset	Somerset
Postcode	TA34 6FT	TA1 6RD
Contact	Joe Adams	Susan Smith
VAT no	444 7774 666	212 5555 456
Telephone	01786-234512	01653-87878
For both, select the Credit Control tab and tick the Terms agreed in the Restrictions section		

The **A/C Code** has to be different for each customer and can be numeric, alphabetic or a mixture.

It pays to think carefully about how to structure the codes to maximise efficiency and to allow additional customers to be added at a later stage (thus numbering them 1, 2, 3, etc., would cause problems if you wanted to insert a new record between 2 and 3).

You can also set up new customers using **New** button that loads the wizard (although this can be a slower method).

New

After returning to the **Customers** screen, you will see the two customers listed (as shown below).

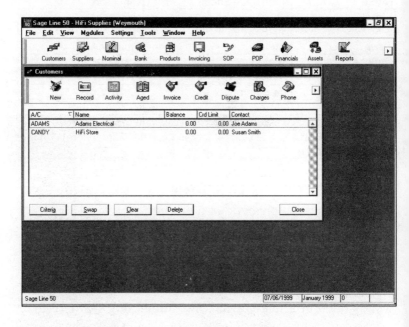

So far, you have entered details of two customers.

The next stage is to enter invoices sent to the customers.

To the right of the **Record** button is the **Invoice** button.

Invoice

This is used to enter details of goods or services you have supplied to customers.

Click the **Invoice** button and you will see a new screen.

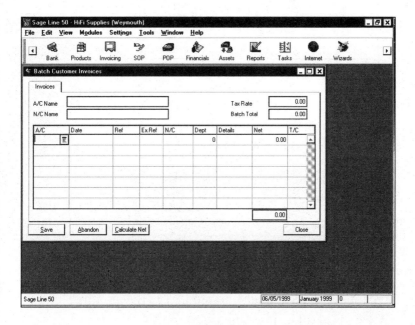

Note the button next to the **A/C** field. This appears within many of the Sage screens. If you click on it, you will see a list of the available data.

Entering Invoice Details

You are going to enter details of two items sold to CANDY.

Some of the data (e.g. the Customer Name) is automatically entered by the program once you have entered the A/C code.

The date can be entered manually or you can use the calendar (by clicking the button).

Accept the **VAT code** as **T1**, this is the default code and is set at the standard rate of VAT (the VAT will be calculated automatically).

Accept the data already entered, e.g. the nominal codes; only add (or alter) the data as required.

Save the invoices by clicking on the **Save** button and click on the **Close** button to return to the main **Customers** screen.

Customer Invoice data to be entered

Both invoices can be entered on the same screen.

You can use the **F6** key to repeat data from the previous line.

A/C (account code)	CANDY	CANDY
Date	01/01/99	09/01/99
Ref	Candy1	Candy2
Description	Aiwa Personal Stereo	Panasonic Personal Stereo
Net	40.00	30.00

You have now entered details of two invoices sent to your customer (CANDY).

Save the data and close the window, returning to the customers screen.

Displaying Account Details

To check the accuracy of your work, use the **Activity** button to show details of the invoices and payments within an account.

Select CANDY by clicking on it so that it is highlighted, then click on the **Activity** button and accept the settings on the dialog box shown below.

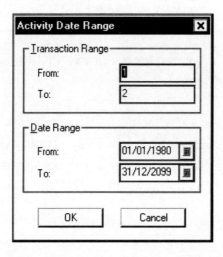

You will see the following screen, showing the invoices you have just entered.

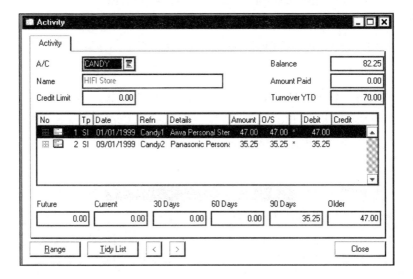

When you are satisfied, **Close** all screens, returning to the main screen. A quick way of achieving this is to pull down the **Window** menu (along the top of the screen) and select **Close All**.

You have now successfully entered customer details and invoices sent to customers. The next stage is to enter details of money received from your customers.

Recording Money Received from Credit Customers

One of the advantages of computerised accounting programs is that when data is entered the double entry book-keeping process is automatic, thus when money is received from customers, both the Sales Ledger and the Bank Account are updated.

Click on the **Bank** button.

Bank

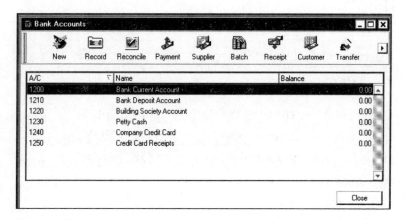

Make sure that the **Bank Current Account** is selected and then click on the **Customers** button.

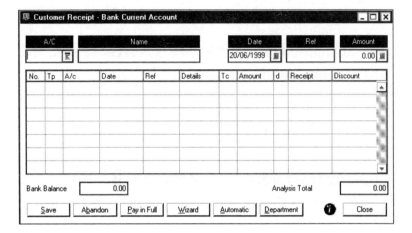

Use the button (next to the **A/C** field) to display the available account codes and choose CANDY from the list shown (clicking on the **OK** button to finish).

The screen will display all the outstanding invoices for the customer.

Alter the **Date** to the 31/01/99.

Click the mouse in the first **Receipt** column (next to the amount for £47.00).

Then click on the **Pay In Full** button.

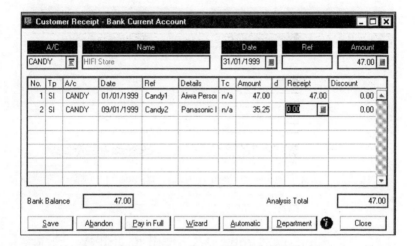

The **Amount** field should automatically show £47.00 and you can then **Save** the payment.

Finally, **Close All** the windows returning to the main Sage screen.

Again, it is worthwhile checking your work by selecting **Customers** (CANDY) and **Activity** to see how the transactions you have posted affect the CANDY account.

Your screen should look similar to that shown.

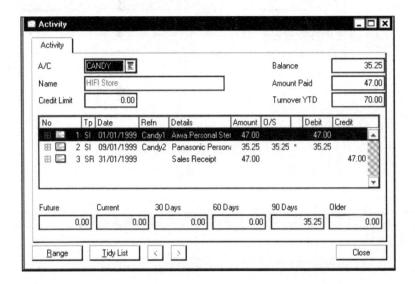

Close all the open windows.

Data and Reports

To finish this section, you can create a report showing the data you have entered.

If you highlight only one item, e.g. one customer, then you will obtain a report on only that item. To create a report on all the items, ensure that none are highlighted.

Within the **Customers** module click on the **Reports** button (you may need to scroll across using the arrowhead button) and you will see the **Customer Reports** dialog box.

Reports

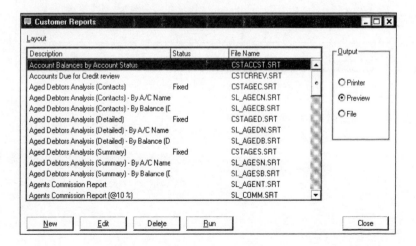

You can see that there are many reports available and you can alter some of them (**Edit**), however the ones marked as **Fixed** cannot be altered.

Select the **Aged Debtors Analysis (Detailed) – By A/C Name** and check that **Preview** is selected, then click on the **Run** button.

Alter the data within the next dialog box to that shown below.

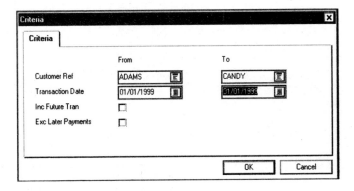

You will see the following summary of the data.

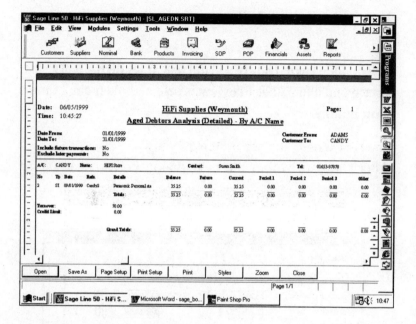

Close all the open windows.

Backing up Your Data

It is best to back up your data files regularly, you will be prompted to do so when exiting the program.

Alternatively you can back up at any time by pulling down the **File** menu and selecting **Backup**.

The first screen you see is shown below.

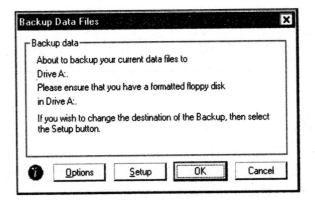

Click the **Setup** button and then choose the **A:** drive (or whatever drive/folder you wish to back up to), clicking **OK** when you have selected the correct drive.

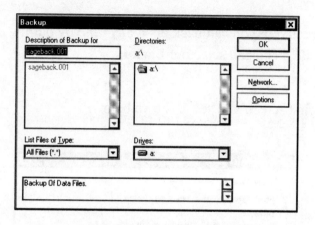

Finally click on **OK** to backup your files.

There is a considerable difference between **Backup** and **Restore** - this is explained in the Appendices.

Summary

So far you have learnt to:

❖ Record details of customers (Record)

❖ Enter invoices into the ledger (Invoices)

❖ Record money received from customers (Bank)

❖ Look at the transactions within a customer account (Activity)

❖ Print out a report (Reports)

❖ Back up your data to a floppy disc (Backup)

Your next step is to practise what you have learnt so far.

Remember to look back if you are unsure.

New data (Customers)

Enter details of a new customer into the ledger.

A/C	MFIRST
Name	Music First
Street1	56B
Street2	Jeremy Street
Town	Bridgewater
County	Somerset
Postcode	TA9 7TR
Contact	Bill Baggins
VAT no	963 2541 777
Telephone	01678-43987
Select the **Credit Control** tab and tick the **Terms Agreed** in the **Restrictions** section	

Enter the following invoices to your customers.

A/C	ADAMS	CANDY
Date	07/01/99	10/01/99
Ref	AD1	Candy3
Description	Aiwa Mini System	Sony SS86 Speakers
Net	200	70

Enter these payments from your customers.

A/C	CANDY	CANDY
Date	31/01/99	31/01/99
Ref	Candy2	Candy3
Paid	35.25	82.25

Close all the open windows.

Check these by using the **Activity** button (in the **Customers** module).

For example, the CANDY (account) should look like this.

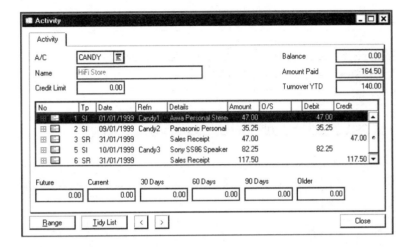

Close all the open windows.

Purchase Ledger

The Purchase Ledger (called **Suppliers** within Sage) is used to record credit purchases.

A credit purchase is when the goods or services are supplied to you and an invoice is received for payment later (normally within a month).

The basic data entered into the Purchase Ledger is:

❖ Suppliers Names, Addresses and other necessary details.

❖ Details of the invoices received for goods or services supplied.

Each supplier is allocated a separate account and each account is given its own account code.

Entering Data into the Purchase Ledger (Suppliers)

After clicking the (left-hand) mouse button on **Suppliers** in the main Sage screen, you will see the **Suppliers** screen.

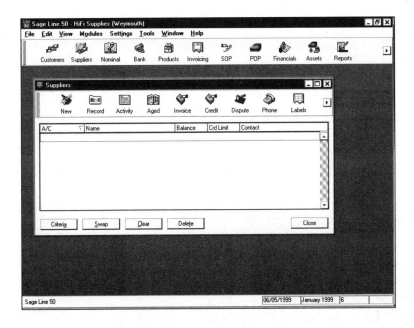

Recording Supplier Details

To begin you have to enter the supplier
details. To do so, click the **Record** button
and the following screen will appear.

Record

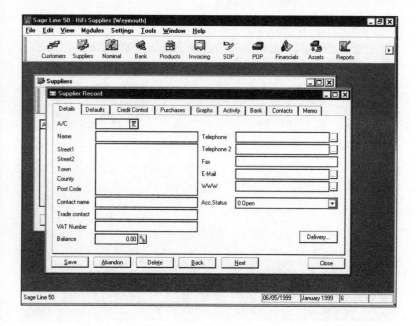

You enter each supplier's details within this screen.

You **must** save each record before moving onto the next; this is done by clicking on the **Save** button along the bottom of the screen. If you make a mess and want to start again just click the **Abandon** button to begin again.

When you have finished entering the suppliers, click on the **Close** button and return to the **Supplier** screen.

Supplier Data to be entered

A/C	CHIMP	FAREAST
Name	Cheap Importers PLC	Far Eastern HiFi Products PLC
Street1	The Old Warehouse	33 Middle Street
Street2	Wareham Industrial Village	
Town	Wareham	Oldtown
County	Dorset	Shropshire
Postcode	BN45 7TR	SH5 3ER
Contact	Ilias Oldround	Oliver Ashbury
VAT No.	666 5454 222	935 4125 789
Telephone	01654 887766	01287 654391
Email	Ilias@chimp.co.uk	oliver@fareast.demon.co.uk
WWW	www.chimp.co.uk	www.fareast.demon.co.uk
For both, select the **Credit Control** tab and tick the **Terms Agreed** in the **Restrictions** section		

The **A/C Code** has to be different for each supplier and can be numeric, alphabetic or a mixture.

In a similar way to the Customers module, you can enter this data using the **New** button, which loads the wizard, but this may be slower.

New

After returning to the **Supplier** screen, you will see the supplier listed (as shown below).

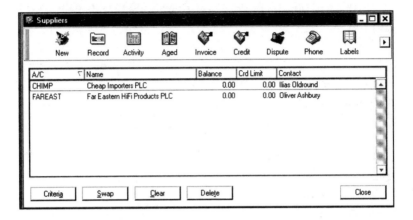

So far, you have entered details of suppliers into the Purchase Ledger.

Entering Invoice Details

The next stage is to enter invoices received from your suppliers.

To the right of the **Record** button is the **Invoice** button.

This is used to enter details of goods or services you have purchased.

Click the **Invoice** button and you will see a new screen.

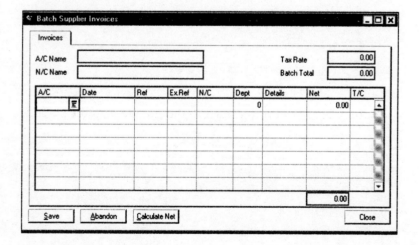

You are going to enter details of items purchased.

Note the magnifying glass button next to the
A/C field.

If you click on it, a list of the available data will be shown
and you can then select from this list.

You can enter the date manually or use the
calendar (by clicking the button).

Accept the **VAT code** as **T1**, this is the default code and is
set at the standard rate of VAT (the VAT will be calculated
automatically), the appendices contain a list of the VAT
codes.

Save the invoices by clicking on the **Save** button and click
on the **Close** button to return to the main **Supplier** screen.

Supplier Invoice Data to be entered

A/C (account code)	CHIMP	FAREAST
Date	01/01/99	01/01/99
Ref	Jan	Jan
Description	20 Aiwa personal stereos	30 Panasonic personal stereos
Net	£400.00	£450.00

You can use the **F6** key to repeat data from one cell to another; this can speed up data entry considerably.

You have now entered details of two invoices sent from your suppliers.

Displaying Account Details

To check the accuracy of your work, you can view details of the invoices and payments within an account.

Select FAREAST (by clicking on it so that it is highlighted), then click on the **Activity** button and accept the settings on the dialog box shown below.

Activity

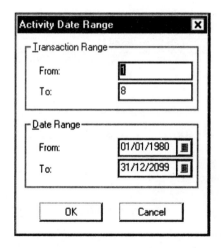

The following screen is displayed, showing the invoice you have just entered.

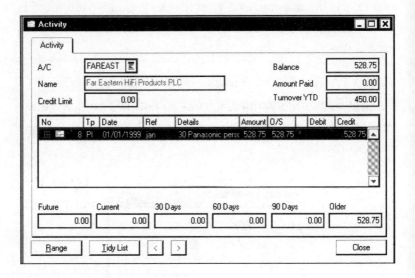

When you are satisfied, **Close** all screens, returning to the main screen.

A quick way of achieving this is to pull down the **Windows** menu (along the top of the screen) and select **Close All**.

You have now successfully entered supplier details and invoices received.

Recording Money Paid to Suppliers

The next stage is to enter details of money paid to your suppliers.

To start this process, click on the **Bank** button.

Make sure that the **Bank Current Account** is selected and then click on the **Supplier** button.

Use the button (next to the **Payee** field) to display the available supplier codes and choose CHIMP from the list shown (clicking on the **OK** button to finish).

The screen will display the outstanding invoice for the supplier.

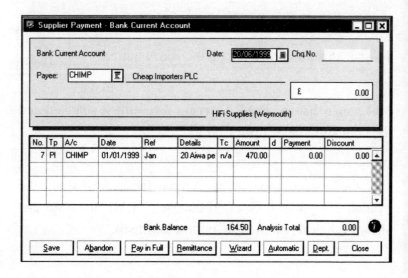

Alter the **Date** to the 31/01/99.

Click the mouse in the **Payment** column (next to the amount for £470.00).

Then click on the **Pay In Full** button.

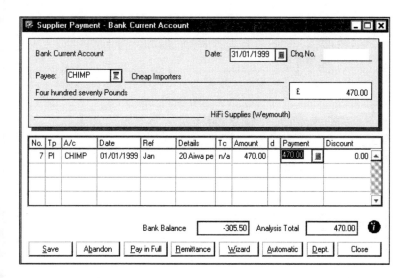

The **Amount** field should automatically show £470.00 and you can then **Save** the payment.

Finally, **Close All** the windows returning to the main Sage screen.

Again, it is worthwhile checking your work by selecting **Suppliers** (highlight CHIMP) and click the **Activity** button to see how the transactions you have posted affect the account.

Your screen should look similar to this.

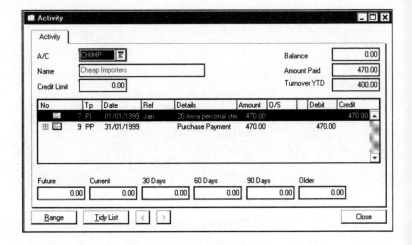

Close all the open windows.

Printing Data and Reports

To finish this section, print out a report showing the data you have entered.

Within the **Suppliers** module click on the **Reports** button (you may need to scroll across using the arrowhead button) and you will see the **Supplier Reports** dialog box.

Reports

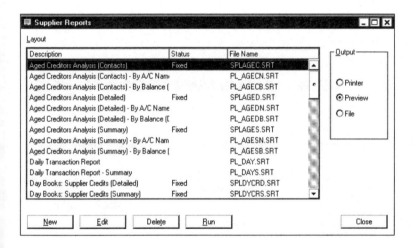

Select the **Aged Creditors Analysis (Contacts)** and check that **Preview** is selected, and then click on the **Run** button.

Alter the data to that shown below.

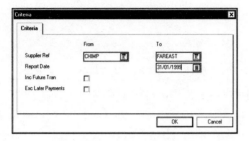

You will see a summary of the data. Close all the open windows.

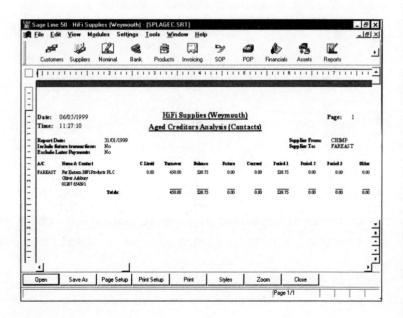

Summary

So far you have learnt to:

❖ Record details of suppliers (Record)

❖ Enter invoices into the ledger (Invoices)

❖ Record money paid to suppliers (Bank)

❖ Look at the transactions within an account (Activity)

❖ Preview a report (Reports)

New data (Suppliers)

Enter details of a new supplier into the ledger.

A/C	CONNECTS
Name	Connections
Street1	87b Oldmile Street
Street2	Newbottom
Town	Truro
County	Cornwall
Postcode	TR7 67R
Contact	Muriel Jenkins
VAT No.	231 8547 699
Telephone	0199 54231
Email	muriel@connects.com
WWW	www.connects.com
Select the **Credit Control** tab and tick the **Terms Agreed** in the **Restrictions** section	

Enter the following invoices, saving when you have entered them.

A/C (account code)	CHIMP	CONNECTS	FAREAST
Date	20/01/1999	21/01/1999	23/01/1999
Ref	jan2	Jan	jan2
Description	15 Aiwa CD players	10 interconnects	5 Panasonic CD players
Net	600.00	100.00	300.00

A/C (account code)	CHIMP	FAREAST
Date	01/01/99	01/01/99
Ref	Jan3	Jan3
Description	Aiwa mini system	Sony ss86 speakers
Net	160.00	45.00

Close the window.

Preview the DayBooks: Suppliers Invoices (Detailed) report.

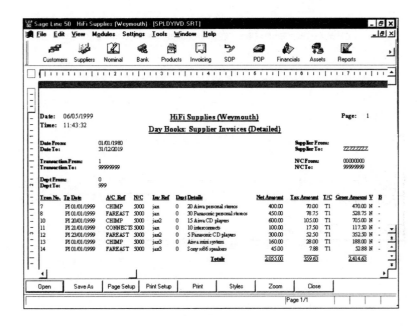

Close all the open windows and enter these **bank** payments
to your suppliers, saving each in turn.

A/C	CHIMP	FAREAST
Date	31/01/99	31/01/99
Ref	Jan2	Jan2
Payment	705.00	352.50

Finally preview the **Aged Creditors Analysis (Detailed) -
By A/C Name** (this is found in the suppliers module).

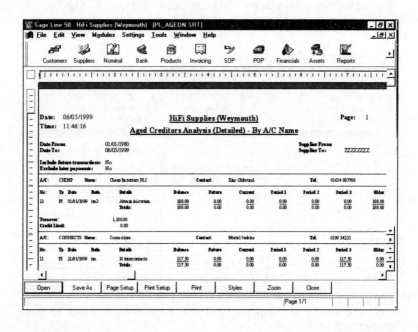

Close all open windows.

New Month - February

You have entered data for the month of January 1999, now to enter data for the month of February.

Look back at the previous examples if you are unsure, you have not covered the correction of errors yet!

Customers Data

Enter these new customers.

A/C	TEMPLE	KENWYN
Name	Templecombe Audio	Kenwyn Supplies
Street1	89 High Street	Summerlands
Street2		SeaView
Town	Templecombe	Falmouth
County	Somerset	Cornwall
Postcode	TE4 6TT	TR8 9HG
Contact	Bill Bastins	Hugo Forest
VAT No.	555 7584 631	921 5362 845
Telephone	01654 783212	01555 621397
Select the **Credit Control** tab and tick the **Terms Agreed** in the **Restrictions** section		

Enter these customer invoices.

A/C (account code)	TEMPLE	KENWYN
Date	12/02/99	15/02/99
Ref	Feb	Feb
Description	2 Panasonic CD players	3 Aiwa CD players
Net	160.00	165.00

A/C (account code)	CANDY	MFIRST
Date	22/02/99	24/02/99
Ref	Feb	Feb
Description	4 Aiwa personal stereos	2 Panasonic personal stereos
Net	160.00	60.00

Enter the following cheques received from your customers.

A/C	TEMPLE	KENWYN
Date	28/02/99	28/02/99
Ref	Feb	Feb
Paid	188.00	193.88

Suppliers Data

Please enter these invoices from your suppliers.

A/C (account code)	CONNECTS	CHIMP	FAREAST
Date	12/02/99	15/02/99	23/02/99
Ref	Feb	Feb	Feb
Description	20 assorted plugs	5 Sony 14" T.V.s	5 Sony VCRs
Net	12.00	350.00	500.00

Now enter these **bank** payments to your suppliers.

A/C	CONNECTS	CHIMP
Date	28/02/99	28/02/99
Ref	Jan	Jan3
Payment	117.50	188.00

Close all the open windows.

Viewing the transactions

Click the **Customers** button and then the **Activity** button (making sure none of the customers is highlighted).

Accept the settings in the **Activity Date Range** dialog box and you will see a display of the transactions for the first customer account.

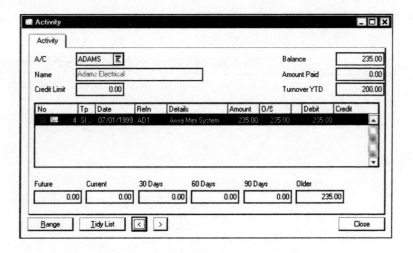

You can scroll through all the customers by clicking the arrow button. Now look at the suppliers' activities.

Products (Stock)

You have entered information about your sales and purchases; another important aspect of your accounts is stock control.

Entering Details of the Products

Begin by recording stock details; these have to be recorded **before** the stock movements can be entered.

To do this, click the **Products** button, followed by **Record** and you will see the following screen (alternatively, you could use the **New** button to load the wizard).

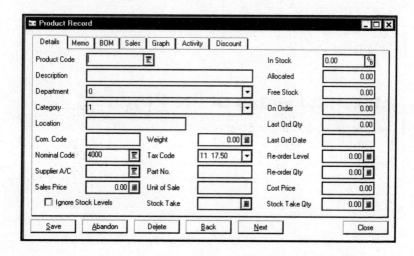

Enter the following data (ignoring and/or accepting any fields not specified).

Save each before proceeding to enter the next.

Product Code	AIWA-MINI	SONY-SP	AIWA-PS
Description	Aiwa mini system	Sony SS86 speakers	Aiwa personal stereo
Supplier A/C	CHIMP	FAREAST	CHIMP
Sale Price	200.00	70.00	40.00
Unit of sale	one	Pair	one
Reorder level	0	0	20
Reorder Quantity	1	1	10

Product Code	PANA-PS	AIWA-CD	INTERC
Description	Panasonic personal stereo	Aiwa CD player	Interconnects
Supplier A/C	FAREAST	CHIMP	CONNECTS
Sale Price	30.00	55.00	2.00
Unit of sale	single	single	Pair
Reorder level	20	10	15
Reorder Quantity	10	5	10

Product Code	PANA-CD	PLUGS	SONY-TV-14
Description	Panasonic CD player	Plugs	Sony 14" T.V.
Supplier A/C	FAREAST	CONNECTS	CHIMP
Sale Price	80.00	1.00	100.00
Unit of sale	single	single	Single
Reorder level	5	20	5
Reorder Quantity	5	10	5

Product Code	SONY-VCR
Description	Sony VCR
Supplier A/C	FAREAST
Sale Price	150.00
Unit of sale	Single
Reorder level	5
Reorder Quantity	5

Close the **Product Record** screen and you will see the products.

Some items are shown in red, this is because the number of items in stock is less than the reorder level.

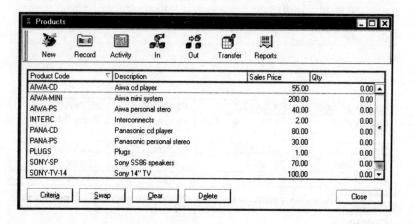

Close down all the open windows.

Entering Stock Movements

Once the stock details have been entered, you can begin to enter stock being purchased or sold.

Stock In

To enter stock movements, select the **Products** button and click the **In** button.

In

Enter the following data and then **Save** it.

Product Code	Details	Date	Ref.	Qty	Cost Price	On order	Free
AIWA-MINI	Aiwa mini system	01/01/1999		1.00	160.00	0.00	0.00
SONY-SP	Sony SS86 speakers	01/01/1999		1.00	45.00	0.00	0.00
AIWA-PS	Aiwa personal stero	01/01/1999		20.00	20.00	0.00	0.00
PANA-PS	Panasonic personal s	01/01/1999		30.00	15.00	0.00	0.00
AIWA-CD	Aiwa cd player	20/01/1999		15.00	40.00	0.00	0.00
INTERC	Interconnects	21/01/1999		10.00	1.00	0.00	0.00
PANA-CD	Panasonic cd player	23/01/1999		5.00	60.00	0.00	0.00
PLUGS	Plugs	12/02/1999		20.00	0.60	0.00	0.00
SONY-TV-14	Sony 14" TV	15/02/1999		5.00	70.00	0.00	0.00
SONY-VCR	Sony VCR	23/02/1999		5.00	100.00	0.00	0.00

Close down the open window, returning to the **Products** screen.

Stock Out

This time select the **Out** button and enter the following data, saving the data after entering it.

Product Code	Details	Date	Ref.	Qty	In stock	On order	Allocated
AIWA-PS	Aiwa personal stereo	01/01/1999		1.00	20.00	0.00	0.00
PANA-PS	Panasonic personal s	09/01/1999		1.00	30.00	0.00	0.00
AIWA-MINI	Aiwa mini system	07/01/1999		1.00	1.00	0.00	0.00
SONY-SP	Sony SS86 speakers	10/01/1999		1.00	1.00	0.00	0.00
PANA-CD	Panasonic cd player	12/02/1999		2.00	5.00	0.00	0.00
AIWA-CD	Aiwa cd player	15/02/1999		3.00	15.00	0.00	0.00

Now enter the following items on a new screen (it is necessary to do this as the program only allows one entry for each item code within each Stock Adjustments screen).

Product Code	Details	Date	Ref.	Qty	In stock	On order	Allocated
AIWA-PS	Aiwa personal stereo	22/02/1999		4.00	19.00	0.00	0.00
PANA-PS	Panasonic personal s	24/02/1999		2.00	29.00	0.00	0.00

Close the open window, returning to the Products screen.

Stock Activity

To view any product's activity, select the product(s) (by highlighting) and then click the **Activity** button, you will see a screen similar to this.

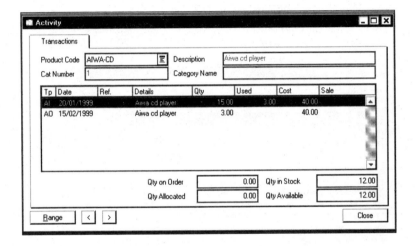

When you have finished, close the window, returning to the Products screen.

Product Reports

Before clicking the **Report** button, be careful to ensure that you do not highlight any of the stock items, otherwise you will only get a report about those (highlighted) items.

There is a variety of product reports, which you can see by clicking on the **Reports** button (see the illustration below).

Reports

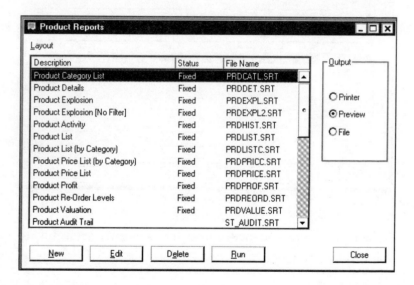

For example if you preview the **Product Activity** report, you will see the products listed in sequence with the stock movements for each.

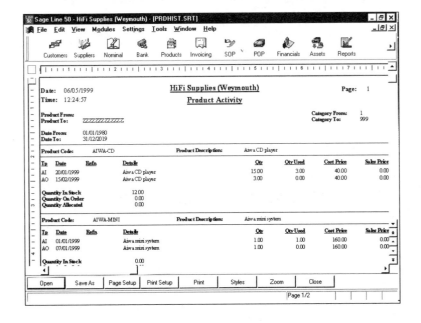

Another useful report is the **Product Valuation** report (illustrated below).

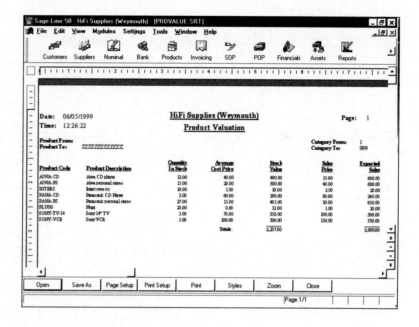

Close all the open windows.

If you have made any mistakes you have to go back to the relevant **Products** screen and alter the data, you cannot use the (**File**) **Maintenance** screen (see appendix) as the products data is not recorded on the audit trail (as financial transactions are).

Summary

So far, you have learnt to:

❖ Record details of products

❖ Enter stock in

❖ Enter stock out

❖ View product reports

The Financials

You have now entered data for sales, purchases and stock for two months.

The next module to investigate is **Financials**. This enables you to produce accounting statements, e.g. Balance Sheets.

One of the advantages of computerised systems will now become evident, the ability to produce financial reports without any material additional effort or time.

Click the **Financials** button.

You are going to view the **Trial Balance**.

To do this, click the **Trial** button and then on the next screen alter the **Period** to month 2, February 1999.

Check that **Preview** is selected.

You should see a screen similar to this.

Date:	30/03/1999	Hi-Fi Supplies (Weymouth)		Page:	1
Time:	12:10:25	Period Trial Balance			

To Period: Month 2, February 1999

N/C	Name		Debit	Credit
1100	Debtors Control Account		493.50	
1200	Bank Current Account			1,286.62
2100	Creditors Control Account			1,594.48
2200	Sales Tax Control Account			154.88
2201	Purchase Tax Control Account		510.48	
4000	Sales Type A			885.00
5000	Materials Purchased		2,917.00	
		Totals:	3,920.98	3,920.98

Close all the open windows.

Adjusting for Stock

In order to show the correct profit, you have to calculate the **cost of sales** (the purchases adjusted for opening and closing stock).

The program will do this for you if you use the **Wizard**, you will not need to use your knowledge of double entry bookkeeping and journals.

The manual journal entries (without using the wizard) are described in the appendices.

Click the **Wizards** button on the (main) toolbar, you will need to scroll to the right to find it, and then select **Opening Closing Stock Wizard**.

You will see the first of several screens, accept this and move to the next.

Here you will be asked to confirm the nominal codes.

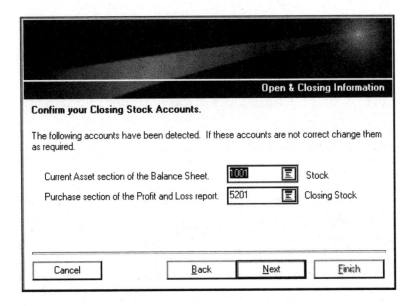

Unless you have altered these, you can move onto the next screen.

Enter the data shown below (always check **the date** as it must be in the month for which you are creating accounts).

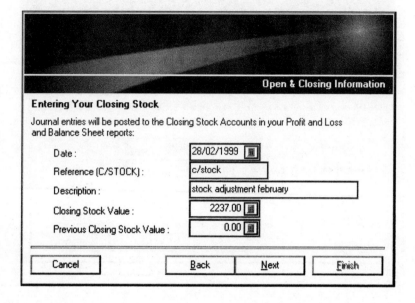

The final screen shows you the journal entries the program will make.

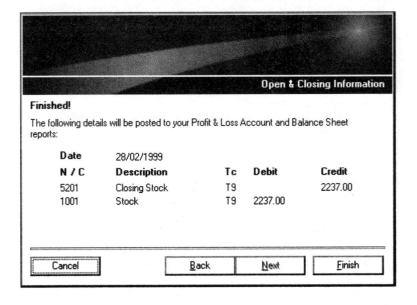

Accept these (if they are correct) and you have adjusted for the opening and closing stock.

The Trading, Profit & Loss Account

It is now a simple matter to produce the accounts, click on the **Financials** button and then on the **P and L** button

Alter the periods on the following screen as shown.

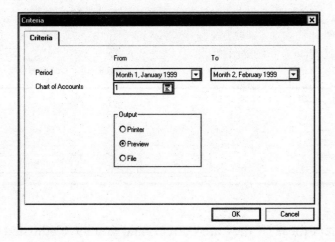

You should now see the profit and loss account for the two-month period.

| Date: 06/05/1999 | | HiFi Supplies (Weymouth) | | Page: 1 |
| Time: 12:57:19 | | Profit & Loss | | |

From: Month 1, January 1999
To: Month 2, February 1999

Chart of Accounts: Default Chart of Accounts

		Period		Year to Date	
Sales					
Product Sales		885.00		885.00	
			885.00		885.00
Purchases					
Purchases		2,917.00		2,917.00	
Stock		(2,237.00)		(2,237.00)	
			680.00		680.00
Direct Expenses					
			0.00		0.00
Gross Profit/(Loss):			205.00		205.00
Overheads					
			0.00		0.00
Net Profit/(Loss):			205.00		205.00

Balance Sheet

To display the Balance Sheet, click the **Balance** button and select the same periods as the Profit and Loss Account.

The previewed result should look like this.

	Period		Year to Date
Fixed Assets			
		0.00	0.00
Current Assets			
Stock	2,237.00		2,237.00
Debtors	493.50		493.50
VAT Liability	355.60		355.60
		3,086.10	3,086.10
Current Liabilities			
Creditors : Short Term	1,594.48		1,594.48
Bank Account	1,286.62		1,286.62
		2,881.10	2,881.10
Current Assets less Current Liabilities:		205.00	205.00
Total Assets less Current Liabilities:		205.00	205.00
Long Term Liabilities			
		0.00	0.00
Total Assets less Total Liabilities:		205.00	205.00
Capital & Reserves			
P&L Account	205.00		205.00
		205.00	205.00

Close all the open windows.

Summary

In this section you have learnt to:

❖ Produce the trial balance

❖ Create journal entries to adjust for opening and closing stock by using the wizard

❖ Produce the Trading, Profit & Loss Account

❖ Produce a Balance Sheet.

New Month (March)

More on Customers and Suppliers

You have entered details of purchases and sales of stock and have recorded the stock itself.

Normally you will want to set up supplier and customer accounts for as many of your customers and suppliers as possible so that you can take advantage of the many reports, etc., that can be accessed from the **Customers** and **Suppliers** modules.

Examples of such items are garage bills, motor expenses, stationery costs, professional fees and so on.

However, you may not want to set up accounts for one-off transactions, e.g. a cash sale.

To practise this, set up the following **Suppliers** accounts.

A/C	JCMOTORS	ULTSTAT
Name	Jacob Cornish Motor Company	Ultimate Stationery Company
Street1	45 Chesire Street	Unit 4
Street2		Harbourside Industrial Park
Town	Weymouth	Weymouth
County	Dorset	Dorset
Postcode	DO8 9TR	DO5 6TR
Contact	Jacob Cornish	Christiana Goodenough
VAT No.	521 7898 217	564 2648 654
Telephone	02541 549874	02541 368742
Email		chris@aol.com
For both, select the **Credit Control** tab and tick the **Terms Agreed** in the **Restrictions** section		

Now record these invoices from the suppliers (note the nominal code for the invoices).

A/C	Date	Ref	Ex.Ref	N/C	Dept	Details	Net	T/C
JCMOTORS	05/03/1999	service		7301	0	yearly service	95.00	T1
ULTSTAT	09/03/1999	paper		7504	0	laser paper	33.99	T1

Record this bank payment (enter the date of the cheque payment as the 31st March) and close all open windows.

Tp	A/c	Date	Ref	Details	Tc	Amount	d	Payment	Discount	
PI	JCMOTOR	05/03/1999	service	yearly servic	n/a	111.63		111.63	0.00	▦

Dealing with Credit Notes

Sometimes you have to issue a credit note, for example, where the customer has returned goods.

Credit Notes from Suppliers

You have returned the **laser paper** to the supplier (ULTSTAT), as faulty.

To account for this, you need to enter the credit note.

Click on the **Suppliers** button and then the **Credit** button.

Credit

Enter the following data and save it.

A/C Name	Ultimate Stationery Company					Tax Rate		17.50
N/C Name	Office Stationery					Batch Total		39.94

A/C	Date	Cd. No	Ex.Ref	N/C	Dept	Details	Net	T/C
ULSTAT	31/03/1999			7504	0	returns	33.99	T1

When you **Close** this window, returning to the **Suppliers** window, you should see the amount for the supplier is zeroed.

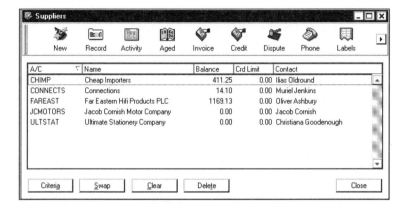

Close all open windows.

Credit Notes to Customers

Click the **Customers** button and then **Credit**.

Credit

Enter the following data (MFIRST are returning all the stock of **Panasonic personal stereos** you sold them).

A/C Name	Music First					Tax Rate		17.50
N/C Name	Sales					Batch Total		70.50

A/C	Date	Crd.No	Ex.Ref	N/C	Dept	Details	Net	T/C
MFIRST	31/03/1999			4000	0	stock returns	60.00	T1

Save this and close the window.

The **Customers** screen should now show the account as having a zero balance.

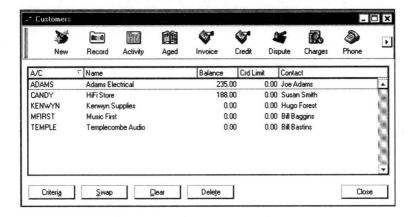

Close the window.

As this is a stock item, you also need to record the item back into stock. Click the **Products** button and then **In**. Record the following data. Save this and close all open windows.

Adjustments In							
Product Code	Details	Date	Ref.	Qty	Cost Price	On order	Free
PANA-PS	Panasonic personal st	31/03/1999	returns	2.00	15.00	0.00	27.00

Other Receipts and Payments

There are some transactions that are not entered in the **Customers** or **Suppliers** modules as they do not have customer or supplier accounts set up for them, instead they are entered using the **Bank** module.

Payments

Use this option to record payments you make that do not involve a supplier account, e.g. payments made from your bank, cash or credit card accounts, examples are wages or miscellaneous payments (e.g. credit card company charges).

Receipts

Used to record money you receive that is not in payment for invoices sent to customers, e.g. cash sales, banking interest.

Entering (Cheque) Payments

Click the **Bank** button and from the next window select **Payment**.

Enter the data shown below, saving when finished.

Note the changes to the **N/C** (nominal code) and the **Tc** (VAT tax codes).

Bank	Date	Ref	N/C	Dept	Details	Net	Tc	Tax
1200	05/03/1999	wages	7005	0	casual wages	45.00	T9	0.00
1200	16/03/1999	bus fare	7400	0	travel	11.99	T0	0.00

Entering Petty Cash Payments

Similarly, enter these petty cash payments.

Bank	Date	Ref	N/C	Dept	Details	Net	Tc	Tax
1230	23/03/1999	cleaning	7801	0	polish	3.83	T1	0.67
1230	26/03/1999	books	7505	0	office97 book	35.00	T0	0.00

Save these and close all the open windows.

Recording Bank Receipts

Select the **Bank** module and then **Receipt**. Enter these receipts.

Receipt

See how you can enter receipts for different (bank or cash) accounts on the same data entry form (this applies to payments as well).

Bank	Date	Ref	N/C	Dept	Details	Net	Tc	Tax
1200	08/03/1999	sale	4000	0	pana pers ster	30.00	T1	5.25
1230	26/03/1999	sale	4000	0	2 plugs	2.00	T1	0.35

You must also record the sales you have just made in the stock records (**Products** module), as they are stock items.

Product Code	Details	Date	Ref.	Qty	In stock
PANA-PS	Panasonic personal ster(	08/03/1999	sale	1.00	29.00
PLUGS	Plugs	26/03/1999	sale	2.00	20.00

Close all open windows.

Transferring Money

It is often necessary to transfer money from one account to another, e.g. from the current bank account to petty cash.

To do this, click the **Bank** button and select **Transfer**.

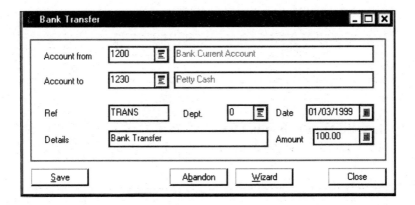

Enter the data as shown above and **Save** it.

This creates a journal entry recording the transfer of the money from one account to the other.

You should now see the following balances.

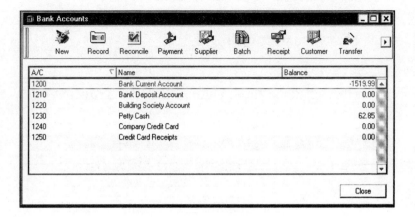

Close all the open windows.

Summary

In this section you have learnt to:

❖ Account for credit notes.

❖ Record bank and cash receipts (and payments)

❖ Record transfers between bank accounts.

End of Period Activities

You printed out various reports for the second period (month 2 - February), you are going to do the same for the 3rd month (March) and also to look at some new reports.

Stock Reorder Lists

One of the reports you may want to look at is a list of stock that needs reordering.

Select the **Products** button and then **Reports**.

Choose the **Purchase Re-order List** and you will see the stock shown where the number of items in stock is below the reorder limits set.

```
Date:  06/05/1999                    HiFi Supplies (Weymouth)                    Page:  1
Time:  13:32:56                        Purchase Re-Order List
```

Supplier From :					Stock Code From :			
Supplier To :	ZZZZZZZ				Stock Code To :	ZZZZZZZ.ZZZZZZZZZZZZ		

Purchase Ref CHIMP   **Name**   Cheap Importers PLC

Stock Code	Description	Qty In Stock	Qty On Order	Qty Allocated	Reorder Lev	Price	Reorder Qty	Value
AIWA-PS	Aiwa personal stereo	15.00	0.00	0.00	20.00	20.00	10.00	200.00
								200.00

Purchase Ref CONNECTS   **Name**   Connections

Stock Code	Description	Qty In Stock	Qty On Order	Qty Allocated	Reorder Lev	Price	Reorder Qty	Value
INTERC	Interconnects	10.00	0.00	0.00	15.00	1.00	10.00	10.00
PLUGS	Plugs	18.00	0.00	0.00	20.00	0.60	10.00	6.00
								16.00

Purchase Ref FAREAST   **Name**   Far Eastern HiFi Products PLC

Stock Code	Description	Qty In Stock	Qty On Order	Qty Allocated	Reorder Lev	Price	Reorder Qty	Value
PANA-CD	Panasonic CD Player	3.00	0.00	0.00	5.00	60.00	5.00	300.00
								300.00
								516.00

Next, preview the **Product Valuation** report.

```
Date:  06/05/1999                    HiFi Supplies (Weymouth)                    Page:  1
Time:  13:34:44                        Product Valuation
```

Product From:				Category From:	1
Product To:	ZZZZZZZZZZ			Category To:	999

Product Code	Product Description	Quantity In Stock	Average Cost Price	Stock Value	Sales Price	Expected Sales
AIWA-CD	Aiwa CD player	12.00	40.00	480.00	55.00	660.00
AIWA-PS	Aiwa personal stereo	15.00	20.00	300.00	40.00	600.00
INTERC	Interconnects	10.00	1.00	10.00	2.00	20.00
PANA-CD	Panasonic CD Player	3.00	60.00	180.00	80.00	240.00
PANA-PS	Panasonic personal stereo	28.00	15.00	420.00	30.00	840.00
PLUGS	Plugs	18.00	0.60	10.80	1.00	18.00
SONY-TV-14	Sony 14" TV	5.00	70.00	350.00	100.00	500.00
SONY-VCR	Sony VCR	5.00	100.00	500.00	150.00	750.00
			Totals:	2,250.80		3,628.00

Close down all the open windows.

Opening and Closing Stock

Preview the **Trial Balance** for **March** (period 3) *before* making the stock adjustments.

Date: 06/05/1999	HiFi Supplies (Weymouth)		Page: 1
Time: 13:37:28	Period Trial Balance		

To Period: Month 3, March 1999

N/C	Name	Debit	Credit
1001	Stock	2,237.00	
1100	Debtors Control Account	423.00	
1200	Bank Current Account		1,519.99
1230	Petty Cash	62.85	
2100	Creditors Control Account		1,594.48
2200	Sales Tax Control Account		149.98
2201	Purchase Tax Control Account	527.78	
4000	Sales Type A		857.00
5000	Materials Purchased	2,917.00	
5201	Closing Stock		2,237.00
7005	Wages - Casual	45.00	
7301	Repairs and Servicing	95.00	
7400	Travelling	11.99	
7505	Books etc.	35.00	
7801	Cleaning	3.83	
	Totals:	**6,358.45**	**6,358.45**

You can see the stocks for the period (codes 1001 & 5201) are shown, these are the opening and closing stock for **February**.

You need to create journal entries to adjust for the **opening stock** and **closing stock** for March.

You can do this using the **Wizard**.

Click on the Wizards button and select **Opening Closing Stock Wizard**.

On the third screen, enter the following data.

Open & Closing Information

Entering Your Closing Stock

Journal entries will be posted to the Closing Stock Accounts in your Profit and Loss and Balance Sheet reports:

Date :	31/03/1999
Reference (C/STOCK) :	c/stock
Description :	adjustment for march
Closing Stock Value :	2250.80
Previous Closing Stock Value :	2237.00

| Cancel | | Back | Next | Finish |

You will then see the following screen asking you to confirm the journal entries.

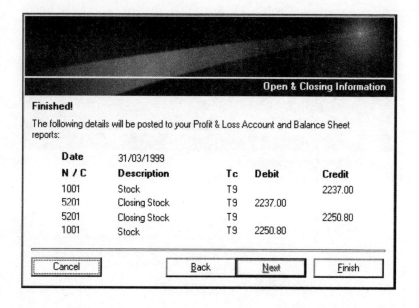

Open & Closing Information

Finished!

The following details will be posted to your Profit & Loss Account and Balance Sheet reports:

Date	31/03/1999			
N / C	**Description**	**Tc**	**Debit**	**Credit**
1001	Stock	T9		2237.00
5201	Closing Stock	T9	2237.00	
5201	Closing Stock	T9		2250.80
1001	Stock	T9	2250.80	

Cancel   <u>B</u>ack   <u>N</u>ext   <u>F</u>inish

Preview the **Trial Balance** for **Period 3 - March**; it should now look like this.

Date: 06/05/1999		HiFi Supplies (Weymouth)	Page: 1	
Time: 13:42:10		Period Trial Balance		
To Period:	Month 3, March 1999			
N/C	Name		Debit	Credit
1001	Stock		2,250.80	
1100	Debtors Control Account		423.00	
1200	Bank Current Account			1,519.99
1230	Petty Cash		62.85	
2100	Creditors Control Account			1,594.48
2200	Sales Tax Control Account			149.98
2201	Purchase Tax Control Account		527.78	
4000	Sales Type A			857.00
5000	Materials Purchased		2,917.00	
5201	Closing Stock			2,250.80
7005	Wages - Casual		45.00	
7301	Repairs and Servicing		95.00	
7400	Travelling		11.99	
7505	Books etc.		35.00	
7801	Cleaning		3.83	
		Totals:	6,372.25	6,372.25

See how the **Trial Balance** reflects the current stock position (code 1001).

Close all the open windows.

Renaming Codes

As you can see from the trial balance, some of the nominal account names are less than helpful.

To alter these, click the **Nominal** button and then **Record**.

Nominal

Alter the following code (names) by either typing in the code or clicking on the button to pull down the list of codes and then selecting the one you want, making the alterations and saving each in turn.

4000	Sales
5000	Purchases

Close all the open windows.

Prepayments and Accruals

A prepayment is when you have paid for an item and the period of the payment extends beyond the accounting period. An adjustment needs to be made otherwise the profit will be understated.

In this case you have paid **breakdown insurance** for the period March to August (and the accounts are only for the three months from Jan to March).

To adjust for this click the **Nominal** button and then the **Prepay** button, enter the following data and save it.

Prepay

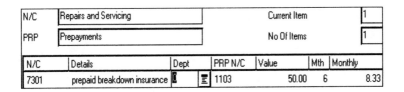

N/C	Repairs and Servicing				Current Item		1
PRP	Prepayments				No Of Items		1
N/C	Details	Dept	PRP N/C	Value		Mth	Monthly
7301	prepaid breakdown insurance		1103	50.00		6	8.33

This sets up the prepayment although it is not posted to the accounts until the **Month End** routines are carried out.

An accrual is where an item (covering a period of time) should have been paid during the accounting period but was actually paid afterwards. If this is not adjusted then the profit will be overstated. Accruals are adjusted in a similar way to Prepayments.

Close all the open windows.

Recurring Payments

These are payments you make regularly, for example standing orders.

To account for these, click the **Bank** button and then **Recurring**.

Click the **Add** button and enter the following data (you are going to start paying rent for your premises on a standing order from March).

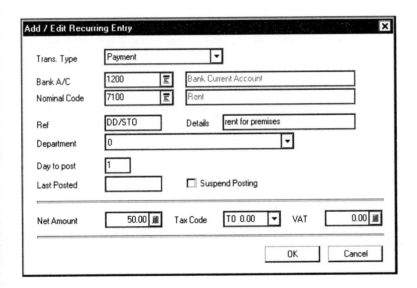

After closing this (by clicking the **OK** button), you should see the **Recurring Entries** window.

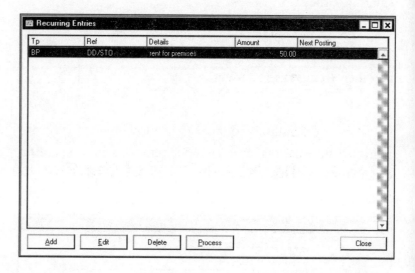

This will not be posted to the accounts until it has been processed (normally at the end of the month).

Close all the open windows.

Fixed Assets

You have to enter fixed assets in the same way you enter any items into the ledgers **and** you also need to set up the depreciation method in the (**Fixed**) **Assets** module.

To Enter the Acquisition of the Fixed Asset

On the 1/3/99 we bought a motorcar from JCMOTORS for £3525 (inc. VAT) on credit.

Enter this in the normal way into the **Suppliers** ledger (as an invoice), but remember the **Nominal Code** should be 0050 (not 5000).

If you enter the full amount in the **Net** column and then click the **Calculate Net** button, the VAT will be calculated for you.

To Record the Depreciation Method

Click the **Assets** button then **Record** and enter the following details (you need to enter the data onto both the **Details** and the **Posting** screens).

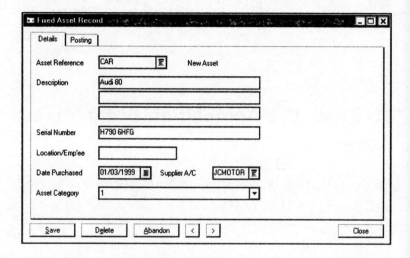

The cost of the asset must be the **Net of VAT** amount.

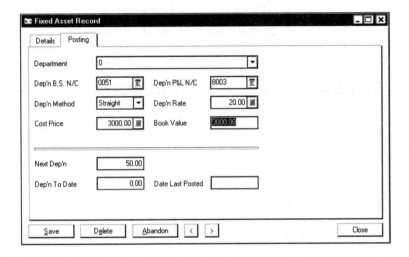

Save the data and close all open windows.

Month End Entries

At the end of every month you need to post the month end adjustments (prepayments, accruals, depreciation) so that they are included in the accounts.

You **MUST** make sure that the **Posting Date** is the last day of the month the accounts are for, otherwise the postings will not be made correctly.

To alter the **Posting Date**, pull down the **Settings** menu and select **Change Program Date**.

In this case alter it to 31/03/1999.

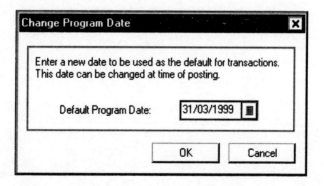

To post the adjustments, pull down the **Tools** menu and select **Period End** and then **Month End**.

Tick the boxes shown below and then the **OK** button.

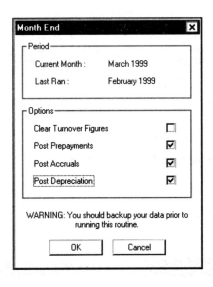

Processing Recurring Entries

Click the **Bank** button and then the **Recurring** button.

Click the **Process** button and you will see the following screen.

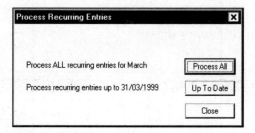

Click the **Process All** button and finally close all the open windows.

You should now alter the **Posting Date** back to the current date before proceeding.

The VAT Return

Most businesses are registered for VAT and
Sage Line 50 will produce your VAT return
without any real effort on your part.

To do this, click the **Financials** button and then **VAT**. You
will see the following screen.

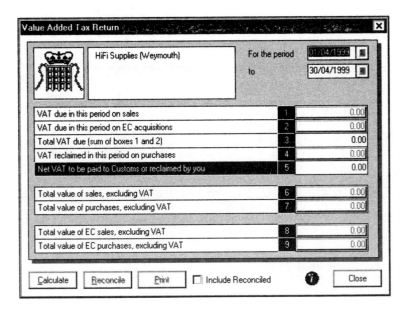

Alter the dates as shown (on the next page) and click the **Calculate** button.

The end result should be similar to this.

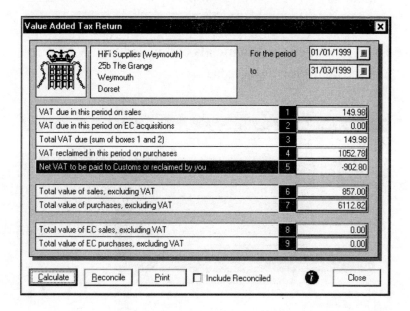

Finally, click the **Reconcile** button (this flags the items that have been included).

At this stage you should transfer the VAT liability from the Sales and Purchase Tax Control Account to the VAT Liability Account (so that the Control Accounts are zeroed to begin the new VAT period).

You use a **Wizard** to do this, click the **Wizards** button, select the **VAT Transfer Wizard** and follow through the screens.

The 2nd screen asks you to confirm the nominal code.

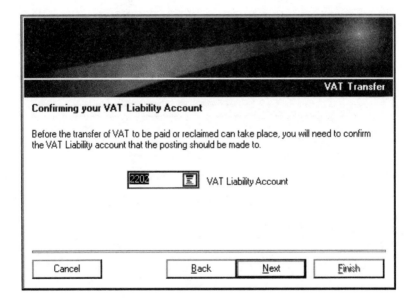

Change the date on the 3rd screen to 31/03/99 and confirm the amounts (from the VAT return you have just completed.

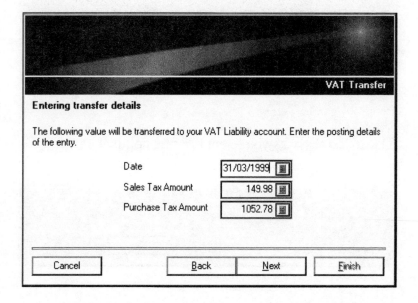

The final screen shows the journal entries that will be made.

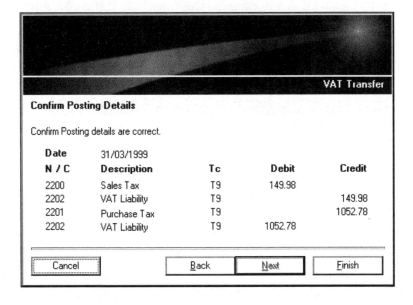

Accept these if you agree with them and **Finish** the wizard.

You have now transferred the sales and purchase VAT to the VAT Liability account.

Close any open windows.

The Trial Balance

If you now click **Financials** button and the **Trial** (Month 3 - March) you will see the revised trial balance, the Sales and Purchase Tax Control Accounts have disappeared (as they contain zero balances).

You should also see new entries for Prepayments (1103) and Vehicle Depreciation (0051).

N/C	Name	Debit	Credit
0050	Motor Vehicles	3,000.00	
0051	Motor Vehicles Depreciation		50.00
1001	Stock	2,250.80	
1100	Debtors Control Account	423.00	
1103	Prepayments	41.67	
1200	Bank Current Account		1,569.99
1230	Petty Cash	62.85	
2100	Creditors Control Account		5,119.48
2202	VAT Liability	902.80	
4000	Sales		857.00
5000	Purchases	2,917.00	
5201	Closing Stock		2,250.80
7005	Wages - Casual	45.00	
7100	Rent	50.00	
7301	Repairs and Servicing	53.33	
7400	Travelling	11.99	
7505	Books etc.	35.00	
7801	Cleaning	3.83	
8003	Vehicle Depreciation	50.00	
	Totals:	9,847.27	9,847.27

The Accounts

Preview the **Profit & Loss A/C** from **Month 1 - January** to **Month 3 - March**.

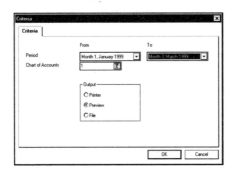

	Period		Year to Date	
Sales				
Product Sales	857.00		857.00	
		857.00		857.00
Purchases				
Purchases	2,917.00		2,917.00	
Stock	(2,250.80)		(2,250.80)	
		666.20		666.20
Direct Expenses				
		0.00		0.00
Gross Profit/(Loss):		190.80		190.80
Overheads				
Gross Wages	45.00		45.00	
Rent and Rates	50.00		50.00	
Motor Expenses	53.33		53.33	
Travelling and Entertainment	11.99		11.99	
Printing and Stationery	35.00		35.00	
Maintenance	3.83		3.83	
Depreciation	50.00		50.00	
		249.15		249.15
Net Profit/(Loss):		(58.35)		(58.35)

Now preview the **Balance Sheet** for the same period.

	Period		Year to Date	
Fixed Assets				
Motor Vehicles	2,950.00		2,950.00	
		2,950.00		2,950.00
Current Assets				
Stock	2,250.80		2,250.80	
Debtors	464.67		464.67	
Deposits and Cash	62.85		62.85	
VAT Liability	902.80		902.80	
		3,681.12		3,681.12
Current Liabilities				
Creditors : Short Term	5,119.48		5,119.48	
Bank Account	1,569.99		1,569.99	
		6,689.47		6,689.47
Current Assets less Current Liabilities:		(3,008.35)		(3,008.35)
Total Assets less Current Liabilities:		(58.35)		(58.35)
Long Term Liabilities				
		0.00		0.00
Total Assets less Total Liabilities:		(58.35)		(58.35)
Capital & Reserves				
P&L Account	(58.35)		(58.35)	
		(58.35)		(58.35)

Close all the open windows.

Looking at the data

As you have seen there are many ways in which you can view the information.

The time saved by having this information easily available is material and is one of the major selling points of this kind of program.

You are now going to investigate more of these.

Customers Data

One of the ways in which you can control your cashflow (and consequently your overall business finances) is by ensuring that your customers pay you promptly.

You can see how much you are owed by your customers and importantly, how long the money has been outstanding by using the **Aged** displays.

Initially click the **Customers** button and then the **Aged** button. Alter the dates to those shown below.

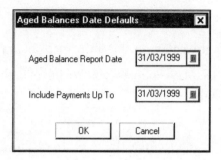

You should see a display like this.

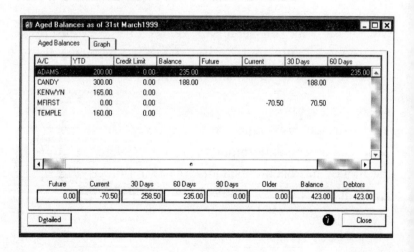

With any date dependent report, the allocation of the balances to the periods depends upon the system date at the time of viewing the report.

As you can see, the debts are shown by period and in total, this type of display enables you to have far more control over your debtors.

You can also display the data as a chart by clicking the **Graph** tab within the window.

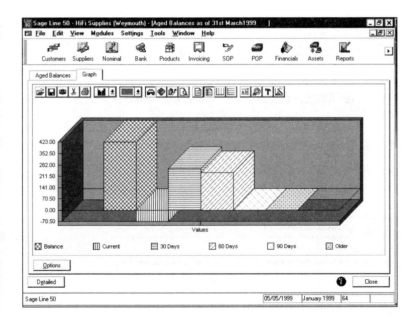

You can alter the way in which the chart is displayed by using the buttons shown along the top of the chart, these are (mostly) standard buttons and enable you to manipulate the chart.

Close all the open windows.

You can also export the chart or copy it to the (Windows) clipboard and then paste it into another program.

Financial Reports

Your accountants should want to see the **Audit Trail**; this is a list of **all** the transactions that have been entered (including any corrections).

Click the **Financials** button and then **Audit**. You want the **Summary** report. On the **Criteria** screen, accept the default entries. The report should look like this.

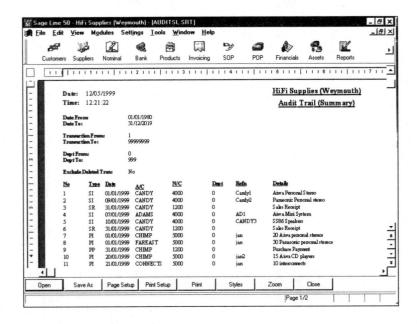

Close all open windows.

Setting up Sage for the first time

Setting up Sage

When you set up Sage for the first time, there are various tasks you need only do once. These include:

❖ Entering your company details

❖ Setting the financial year

❖ Renaming and/or altering the nominal codes

In addition, if an existing business is transferring to Sage

❖ Entering your customers and suppliers details and amounts owed

❖ Entering the opening balances (opening trial balance)

Most of these can be carried out using **Wizards**.

You are going to practise these tasks using dummy data; it is vital that you **REBUILD** your data files **before** and **after** this practice.

This a totally separate exercise to the one at the start of the book and when beginning (and ending) each you should **REBUILD** your data files to remove all the practice data after backing up if you want to keep the data.

Rebuilding (clearing) the data

Before beginning this exercise, clear all the previous data (**after backing it up if necessary**) by pulling down the **File** menu and selecting **Maintenance**.

Click the **Rebuild** button.

Make sure all the ticks are removed from the boxes and this will clear all the existing data.

Next you will be prompted for the financial year, set it to **January 1999**.

Close all the open windows.

Easy Startup Wizard

Click on the **Wizards** button (you may need to scroll to the right to see it) and then select **Easy Startup Wizard**.

Follow through the screens, clicking **Next**, adding or altering the screens as described. If no changes are shown, accept the default settings.

Company Records

The wizard enables you to set the defaults for your business (most of which can be altered later).

These deal with information about your business.

Enter the data shown (if necessary).

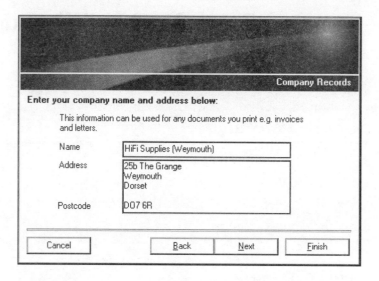

Company Records

Enter your company name and address below:

This information can be used for any documents you print e.g. invoices and letters.

Name	HiFi Supplies (Weymouth)
Address	25b The Grange Weymouth Dorset
Postcode	DO7 6R

Cancel		Back	Next	Finish

Company Records

Company contact numbers.

Enter your company's e-mail address, web site, telephone and fax numbers in the boxes provided.

Web site	www.hifiweym.co.uk
E-Mail	david@hifiweym.co.uk
Telephone	02541 889977
Fax	02541 823309

Cancel		Back	Next	Finish

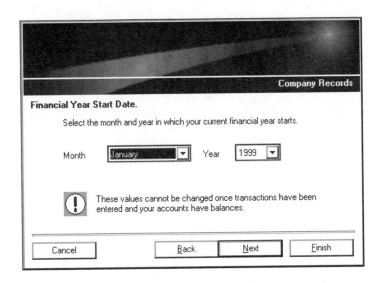

Company Records

Financial Year Start Date.

Select the month and year in which your current financial year starts.

Month [January ▼]   Year [1999 ▼]

These values cannot be changed once transactions have been entered and your accounts have balances.

| Cancel | | Back | Next | Finish |

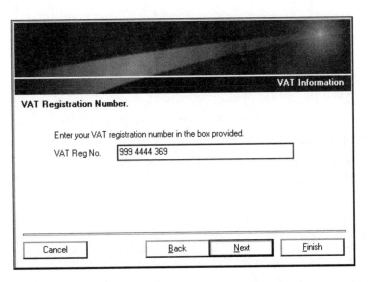

VAT Information

VAT Registration Number.

Enter your VAT registration number in the box provided.

VAT Reg No. [999 4444 369]

| Cancel | | Back | Next | Finish |

VAT Cash Accounting

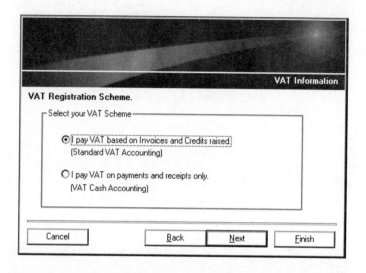

VAT cash accounting means that you pay and reclaim VAT only on the money received or paid. This differs from the standard scheme where you have to pay VAT on sales or purchases when you make the sale or purchase, **not** when you actually pay for the item or receive the money for the sale.

VAT cash accounting is designed to ease the cashflow of small businesses and if you feel it would be useful to you, and then you should contact the VAT office.

Customer & Supplier Information

When setting up the defaults for your customers and suppliers, you can alter the settings, e.g. ageing periods, account terms, nominal codes and VAT rates.

The defaults are set as the standard for all customers and suppliers; you can change individual customer or supplier details (within the respective modules).

The idea is that if much of the information is common then you can enter it here and avoid having to enter it for every individual customer or supplier.

Set the **Payment Due Days** to 30 (days) for both suppliers and customers (as shown).

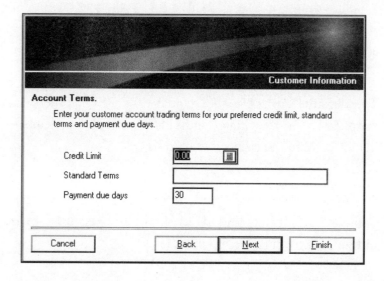

Finally view the remaining screens and **Finish** the wizard.

Customising the Nominal Codes

You can see the list of default nominal codes in the appendices; these can be altered to fit with your company's business.

It is one of the strengths of modern accounting programs that you can easily customise the codes to suit your own personal needs, previously if you needed to do this you would have had to purchase a bespoke program written purely for your business at great expense.

To Change the Name of a Nominal Code

Click the **Nominal** button and then **Record**. You will see the following screen, type in the code you want to alter and make the necessary changes, **saving** each before moving onto the next.

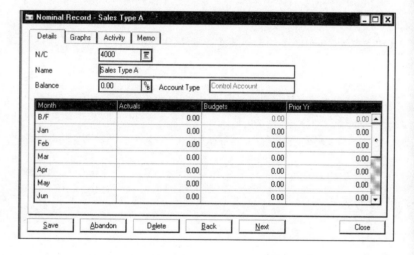

Make the following changes to the codes.

0020	Test Equipment
0021	Test Equipment Depreciation
3000	Capital
4000	Sales
4001	Sales - Connectors
5000	Purchases
5001	Purchases - Connectors
7600	Solicitors Fees
7601	Accountancy Fees

Close down the open window returning to the **Nominal Ledger** window.

Delete the following codes (as they are no longer necessary).

You can do this globally by clicking all the required codes and then clicking the **Delete** button.

0010	Freehold Property
0011	Leasehold Property
1002	Work in Progress
1003	Finished Goods

You can enter them again by using the **Record** button (they are reinstated when you rebuild your files).

You should now see the altered codes.

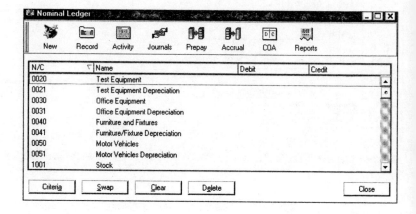

Altering the Chart of Accounts (COA)

You can add new codes to the list, however be very careful to make sure that they are within the correct category for the type of account, i.e. all overheads are between code 7000 and 9999.

You can see the display by clicking the **COA** button and then the **Edit** button.

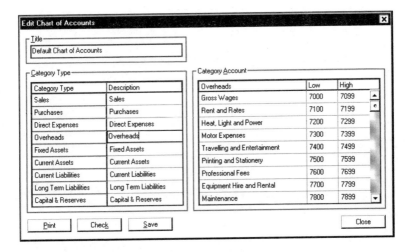

The **COA** shows the allocation of codes for each type of income and expenditure. You can alter the descriptions and the low and high parameters for each range.

> Before altering the default **COA**, please be very careful indeed, only someone who knows the program well and who has an excellent understanding of accounting and bookkeeping should do this.

Close all the open windows.

Existing Customer Accounts

You need to enter existing customer accounts and record the amounts each customer owes to you.

To do this, click the **Customers** button and then **New**.

New

Follow through the wizard, entering the data shown below.

Name	Disco Divahs	The Radio Shop
A/C	DISCODIV	RADIO
Street1	87 Ormond Road	5 High Road
Street2		
Town	Bridgnorth	Helston
County	Shropshire	Cornwall
Postcode	TL8 76Y	HE7 5E
Telephone	01658 963852	0189 789541
Email	chris@divas.freeserve.co.uk	
WWW	www.divas.freeserve.co.uk	
Contact Name	chris glidwell	alfred buttons
Account opened	13/11/1998	01/09/1998
Opening balances (as individual transactions - ignore that the date is outside the current year)		
Reference	Turnt	Cables
Date	13/12/98	12/12/98
Gross	350.00	26.98

Returning to the **Customers** screen, you should see the following display.

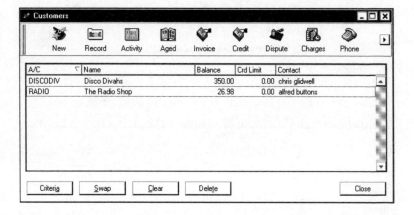

Close all the open windows.

Existing Supplier Accounts

You need to create the accounts and enter the amounts you owe.

To do this, click the **Suppliers** button and then **New**.

Follow through the wizard, entering the data shown below

Name	Japanese Co
A/C	JAPANESE
Street1	6B Yellowstone Industrial Park
Street2	
Town	Lancaster
County	Lancs
Postcode	LA9 7T
Telephone	01333 546982
Email	jojo@japan99.aol.com
WWW	
Contact Name	Joseph Jodphurs
Account opened	08/10/1998
Opening balances (as individual transactions - ignore that the date is outside the current year)	
Reference	Various
Date	25/11/98
Gross	265.21

You should see the following display when finished.

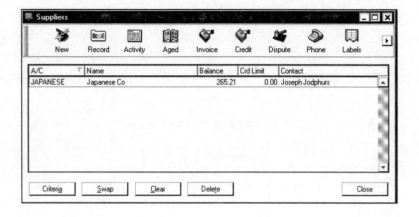

Close all the open windows.

Clearing the Suspense Account

Once you have entered the outstanding customer and supplier balances, you must clear the balance on the Suspense Account (created as a result of entering the balances). Click the **Financials** button and then **Trial**, select **Preview** (as shown below).

You will now see the balances shown for the customer (debtors) and supplier (creditors) invoices you have entered.

Date:	13/05/1999	HiFi Supplies (Weymouth)		Page:	1
Time:	13:22:35	Period Trial Balance			
To Period:	Brought forward				
N/C	**Name**		**Debit**		**Credit**
1100	Debtors Control Account		376.98		
2100	Creditors Control Account				265.21
9998	Suspense Account				111.77
		Totals:	376.98		376.98

To remove these balances (but leaving the outstanding invoices showing in the **Customers** and **Suppliers** modules), you need to create a **Journal**.

Journals

Click the **Nominal** button and then **Journals**.

Enter the following data (see how it is entered as the opposite of the entries in the Trial Balance, this is so it cancels out the original entries).

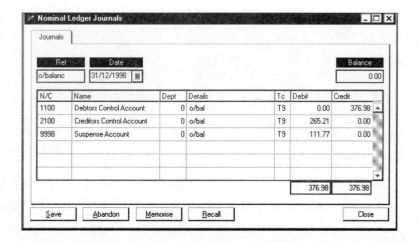

After entering the data, save it.

This clears the nominal balances but leaves the outstanding amounts shown.

To check, click on **Customers** (and **Suppliers**) and you will still see the outstanding amounts.

Close all the open windows.

The Opening Trial Balance

The information you are to enter is from your previous
system (manual or computerised) and is made up of the
balances on the various accounts at the end of the previous
financial year.

To enter these using the journal, click the
Nominal button and then **Journals**.

Enter the data shown below (you will not be able to **Save**
the journal entries unless the journal balances, i.e. the total
debits are equal to the total credits).

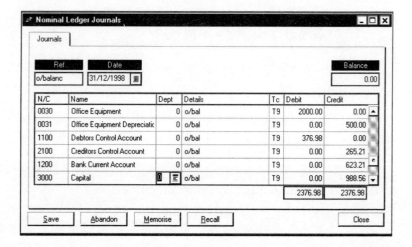

Do not worry about the messages that the date falls outside the current year, it does since you are entering the balances at the end of the previous year.

Close down all the open windows.

Now check what you have achieved by clicking the **Financials** button and then **Trial**.

Set the period to **Brought Forward** and your opening trial balance should look like this.

Date: 29/06/1999 Time: 15:53:34	HiFi Supplies (Weymouth) Period Trial Balance		Page: 1
To Period:	Brought forward		
N/C	**Name**	**Debit**	**Credit**
0030	Office Equipment	2,000.00	
0031	Office Equipment Depreciation		500.00
1100	Debtors Control Account	376.98	
1200	Bank Current Account		623.21
2100	Creditors Control Account		265.21
3000	Capital		988.56
	Totals:	2,376.98	2,376.98

You can now begin to enter the current year's data.

The Appendices

Appendix one

Stock journals

This section deals with how to create your own journals for the opening and closing stock adjustments (if you do not want to use the wizard).

These examples relate to the first exercise (the tutorial).

Adjusting for Opening and Closing Stock (Feb)

In order for your accounts to show the correct profit, you have to calculate the **cost of sales** (the purchases adjusted for opening and closing stock).

The program contains template journals so your knowledge and ability at double entry bookkeeping is not required to the same extent it used to be.

Preview the product valuation report to obtain a stock valuation.

The next stage is to click on the **Nominal** button and then **Journals**.

Journals

You will see the following screen.

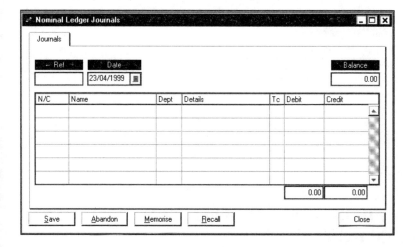

Next click the **Recall** button, select the **Closing Stock Journal** CLSTKJNL.NJR (from the list) and enter the following data (make sure the **date** is correct otherwise the journal will be posted to the wrong month).

N/C	Name	Dept	Details	Tc	Debit	Credit
	Ref	Date				Balance
CLSTKJNL	28/02/1999					0.00
5201	Closing Stock	0	Closing Stock - feb	T9	0.00	2237.00
1001	Stock	0	Closing Stock - feb	T9	2237.00	0.00

Save the journal and you will have adjusted for the closing stock.

Adjusting for Opening and Closing Stock (March)

Since you adjusted for the closing stock at the end of period 2 - February, you need to make two journals, one for the opening stock and the other for the closing stock for the month.

At this stage look at the **Trial Balance** for **March** (period 3) *before* making the stock (or other) adjustments.

```
Date:   06/05/1999                    HiFi Supplies (Weymouth)              Page:   1
Time:   13:37:28                        Period Trial Balance

To Period:      Month 3, March 1999

N/C         Name                                          Debit          Credit
1001        Stock                                       2,237.00
1100        Debtors Control Account                       423.00
1200        Bank Current Account                                        1,519.99
1230        Petty Cash                                     62.85
2100        Creditors Control Account                                   1,594.48
2200        Sales Tax Control Account                                     149.98
2201        Purchase Tax Control Account                  527.78
4000        Sales Type A                                                  857.00
5000        Materials Purchased                         2,917.00
5201        Closing Stock                                               2,237.00
7005        Wages - Casual                                 45.00
7301        Repairs and Servicing                          95.00
7400        Travelling                                     11.99
7505        Books etc.                                     35.00
7801        Cleaning                                        3.83
                                          Totals:        6,358.45        6,358.45
```

You can see the stocks for the period (code 1001 & 5201),
these are the opening and closing stock for **February**.

You need to create journal entries to show:

❖   The **opening stock** for the period

❖   The **closing stock** for the period

Click the **Nominal** button and select **Journal**.

Opening Stock Adjustment

Use the **Recall** button to recall the **Reverse Closing Stock Journal (REVCLSTK.NJR)** and enter the following data.

It is important to ensure that you date the journal within the period you are dealing with, in this case 31st March.

Ref	Date						Balance
REVCLSTK	31/03/1999						0.00

N/C	Name	Dept	Details	Tc	Debit	Credit
1001	Stock	0	Zero feb Closing Stock	T9	0.00	2237.00
5201	Closing Stock	0	Zero feb Closing Stock	T9	2237.00	0.00

Closing Stock Adjustment

Create a journal entry for the closing stock at the end of March by recalling the **Closing Stock Journal (CLSTKJNL.NJR)** and entering the following data, again it is **important** to date the journal entry the 31st March.

Ref	Date					Balance
CLSTKJNL	31/03/1999					0.00

N/C	Name	Dept	Details	Tc	Debit	Credit
5201	Closing Stock	0	Closing Stock - mar	T9	0.00	2250.80
1001	Stock	0	Closing Stock - mar	T9	2250.80	0.00

Preview or print out the **Trial Balance** for **Period 3 - March**.

Date:	06/05/1999	HiFi Supplies (Weymouth)		Page:	1
Time:	13:42:10	Period Trial Balance			

To Period: Month 3, March 1999

N/C	Name	Debit	Credit
1001	Stock	2,250.80	
1100	Debtors Control Account	423.00	
1200	Bank Current Account		1,519.99
1230	Petty Cash	62.85	
2100	Creditors Control Account		1,594.48
2200	Sales Tax Control Account		149.98
2201	Purchase Tax Control Account	527.78	
4000	Sales Type A		857.00
5000	Materials Purchased	2,917.00	
5201	Closing Stock		2,250.80
7005	Wages - Casual	45.00	
7301	Repairs and Servicing	95.00	
7400	Travelling	11.99	
7505	Books etc.	35.00	
7801	Cleaning	3.83	
	Totals:	6,372.25	6,372.25

See how the **Trial Balance** reflects the current stock position (code 1001).

Appendix two

Audit trail types of transaction

BR	Bank receipt
BP	Bank payment
CR	Cash receipt
CP	Cash payment
JD	Journal debit
JC	Journal credit
SI	Sales invoice
SR	Sales receipt
SA	Sales receipt on account
SC	Sales credit note
SD	Discount on sales receipt
PI	Purchase invoice
PP	Purchase payment
PC	Purchase credit note
PD	Discount on purchase payment
PA	Purchase payment on account
VP	Credit payment
VR	Credit receipt

Appendix three

Correcting Mistakes

One of the most common problems is knowing how to correct mistakes or errors. We all make mistakes now and again.

What follows is a guide to the correction of errors.

The majority of mistakes can be corrected using the **File** (pull down menu) and selecting **Maintenance**. As you can see from the illustration, there are four alternatives.

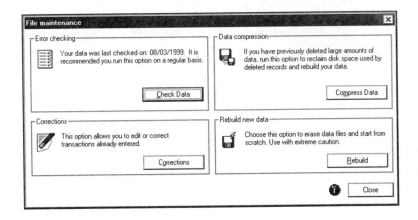

There are some errors or mistakes which require a journal entry to correct, or are mistakes to do with the stock (**Products**), which have to be adjusted within the **Products** module.

Error checking

This checks the data you have entered for inconsistencies or corruption.

Once you have run this you will see a report detailing any problems encountered.

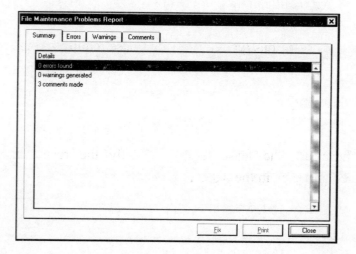

You can use the **Fix** button (if available for the particular problem) to remedy the situation.

The kind of errors that occur include values outside the limits set by the program, transactions that do not match properly, missing or corrupt files or invalid nominal codes.

Warnings

More serious than comments, these should be investigated and dealt with.

Errors

The most serious type of problem, these require fixing.

Comments

These are the least serious, usually the result of an inconsistency in the data.

Corrections

If you have entered data incorrectly, it is often possible to correct the individual item by using this button.

You will see a list of all the transactions and you highlight the one you want to correct and then **Edit** it.

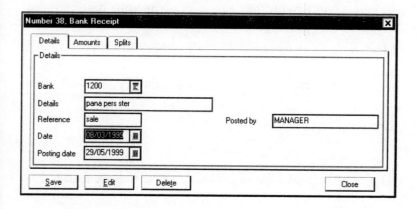

Unfortunately, not all errors can be corrected in this way.

Deleted items are shown in red in the audit trail.

Data compression

This clears space on your disc previously occupied by data you have deleted.

Rebuild new data

Be very careful with this, you will clear your data (so you can begin again).

Ideal when practising but not necessarily a good idea otherwise.

Appendix four

The Nominal Codes

Here are the complete (default) nominal codes.

0010	Freehold Property		2220	Net Wages
0011	Leasehold Property		2230	Pension Fund
0020	Plant and Machinery		2300	Loans
0021	Plant/Machinery Depreciation		2310	Hire Purchase
0030	Office Equipment		2320	Corporation Tax
0031	Office Equipment Depreciation		2330	Mortgages
0040	Furniture and Fixtures		3000	Ordinary Shares
0041	Furniture/Fixture Depreciation		3010	Preference Shares
0050	Motor Vehicles		3100	Reserves
0051	Motor Vehicles Depreciation		3101	Undistributed Reserves
1001	Stock		3200	Profit and Loss Account
1002	Work in Progress		4000	Sales Type A
1003	Finished Goods		4001	Sales Type B
1100	Debtors Control Account		4002	Sales Type C
1101	Sundry Debtors		4009	Discounts Allowed
1102	Other Debtors		4100	Sales Type D
1103	Prepayments		4101	Sales Type E
1200	Bank Current Account		4200	Sales of Assets
1210	Bank Deposit Account		4400	Credit Charges (LP)
1220	Building Society Account		4900	Miscellaneous Income
1230	Petty Cash		4901	Royalties Received
1240	Company Credit Card		4902	Commissions Received
1250	Credit Card Receipts		4903	Insurance Claims
2100	Creditors Control Account		4904	Rent Income
2101	Sundry Creditors		4905	Distribution and Carriage
2102	Other Creditors		5000	Materials Purchased
2109	Accruals		5001	Materials Imported
2200	Sales Tax Control Account		5002	Miscellaneous Purchases
2201	Purchase Tax Control Account		5003	Packaging
2202	VAT Liability		5009	Discounts Taken
2210	P.A.Y.E.		5100	Carriage
2211	National Insurance		5101	Import Duty

5102	Transport Insurance
5200	Opening Stock
5201	Closing Stock
6000	Productive Labour
6001	Cost of Sales Labour
6002	Sub-Contractors
6100	Sales Commissions
6200	Sales Promotions
6201	Advertising
6202	Gifts and Samples
6203	P.R. (Literature & Brochures)
6900	Miscellaneous Expenses
7000	Gross Wages
7001	Directors Salaries
7002	Directors Remuneration
7003	Staff Salaries
7004	Wages - Regular
7005	Wages - Casual
7006	Employers N.I.
7007	Employers Pensions
7008	Recruitment Expenses
7009	Adjustments
7010	SSP Reclaimed
7011	SMP Reclaimed
7100	Rent
7102	Water Rates
7103	General Rates
7104	Premises Insurance
7200	Electricity
7201	Gas
7202	Oil
7203	Other Heating Costs
7300	Fuel and Oil
7301	Repairs and Servicing
7302	Licences
7303	Vehicle Insurance
7304	Miscellaneous Motor Expenses
7350	Scale Charges
7400	Travelling
7401	Car Hire
7402	Hotels
7403	U.K. Entertainment

7404	Overseas Entertainment
7405	Overseas Travelling
7406	Subsistence
7500	Printing
7501	Postage and Carriage
7502	Telephone
7503	Telex/Telegram/Facsimile
7504	Office Stationery
7505	Books etc.
7600	Legal Fees
7601	Audit and Accountancy Fees
7602	Consultancy Fees
7603	Professional Fees
7700	Equipment Hire
7701	Office Machine Maintenance
7800	Repairs and Renewals
7801	Cleaning
7802	Laundry
7803	Premises Expenses
7900	Bank Interest Paid
7901	Bank Charges
7902	Currency Charges
7903	Loan Interest Paid
7904	H.P. Interest
7905	Credit Charges
8000	Depreciation
8001	Plant/Machinery Depreciation
8002	Furniture/Fitting Depreciation
8003	Vehicle Depreciation
8004	Office Equipment Depreciation
8100	Bad Debt Write Off
8102	Bad Debt Provision
8200	Donations
8201	Subscriptions
8202	Clothing Costs
8203	Training Costs
8204	Insurance
8205	Refreshments
9998	Suspense Account
9999	Mispostings Account

Appendix five

Keyboard Shortcuts

F1	The on-line help system.
F2	The calculator; you can paste the result
F4	Displays a pull down menu or list within a data entry window
F5	To paste the current (system date) into a date field
F6	To duplicate a cell - very useful when entering data
F7	To insert a row
F8	To delete a row (useful if you enter a row of data accidentally)
F9	To Calculate Net (of VAT)
F11	To launch the Windows control panel
F12	Minimises the program

Appendix six

VAT Codes

The (default) VAT codes set-up when you install the program are:

T0	zero rated transactions
T1	standard rate
T2	exempt transactions
T4	sales to customers in EC
T7	zero rated purchases from suppliers in EC
T8	standard rated purchases from suppliers in EC
T9	transactions not involving VAT

Appendix seven

Help

Sage Line 50 contains a series of help screens. These are organised in a similar way to other Windows programs with hypertext links.

The help screens are accessed by either pulling down the **Help** menu or by clicking the **Help** button at the end of the main toolbar.

How to find help

Initially you choose either the **Help Contents** or **Library Contents** from the choices.

Help

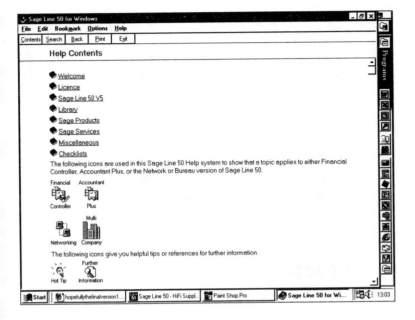

Library

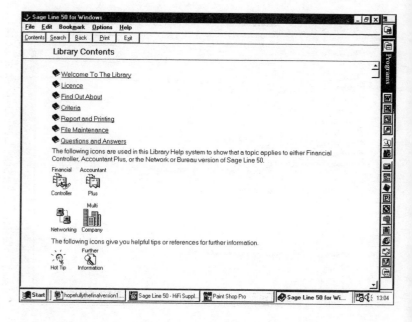

If you click on any of the topics listed (on either of the two previous screens) you will obtain a further list of topics (which are also clickable to either get another list of topics or to display the relevant help screen).

An example of the topics lists is shown below.

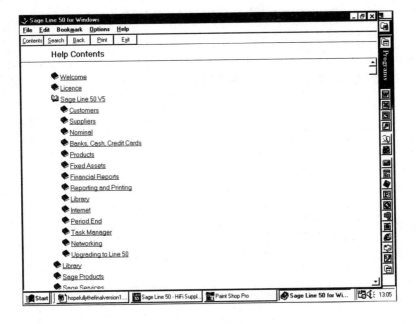

One of the actual help screens (Internet) is illustrated below, many help screens contain hyperlinks which you can click to go to another topic or which explain a word or phrase.

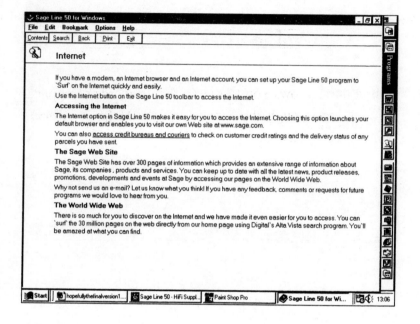

All links are normally shown in green and underlined.

Using the Search button

Along the top of the **Help** or **Library Contents** are a series of buttons, one of which is the **Search** button.

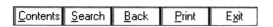

Using these allows you to search for keywords as opposed to working through the lists within the **Help** or **Library Contents** screens.

If you click on the **Search** button, you will display the following dialog box.

You enter the keyword(s) and the program will find the topic closest to the word(s) you entered. Then click the **Display** button and you will see the help on that topic.

Personally I find the **Index** search quick and easy, however for certain topics the **Find** search is more exhaustive and effective if slightly slower in execution.

Appendix eight

Backup and Restore

These are **very** different and if you confuse them, you could end up in a terrible mess.

Backup

This copies the data from your hard disc onto a floppy disc.

It is **vital** to back up your data files regularly and you will be prompted to do so when exiting the program.

You can back up at any time by pulling down the **File** menu and selecting **Backup**.

Whichever method you use, the first screen you see is shown below.

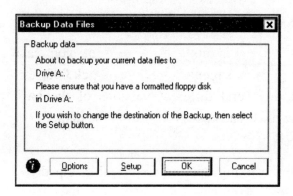

Click the **Setup** button and then choose the **A:** drive (or whatever drive/folder you wish to back up to).

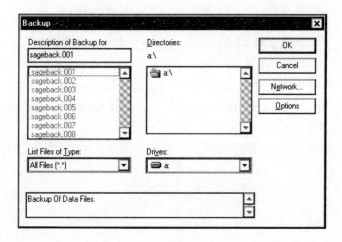

Finally click on **OK**.

The files are saved as **sageback.001**.

However they is nothing to prevent you saving your backup files as **sageback.002**, **sageback.003**, etc., so that you have several different versions of the backup each saved at different stages of entering the data.

I suggest backing up to a floppy disc, zip drive, or tape streamer, etc.

It is important **not** to back up to the same hard disc your data is currently held on (usually the **C:** drive).

The whole point of backing up is to have viable data files to restore from if the original files are corrupted or lost, e.g. if the hard disc becomes unreadable (in which case the backups are likely to be irretrievable if saved to that same hard disc).

The Options button

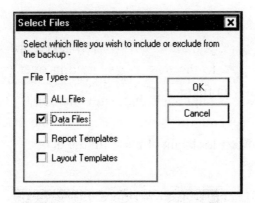

The default is only to back up the data files, if you want to back up any of the other file types then you need to click (tick) the relevant boxes.

Restore

This is the opposite of backing up, when you restore from the floppy disc, you are copying the (backed up) data from the floppy disc to the hard drive, writing over (replacing) the original data files.

The first screen looks like this.

173

Please read the warning carefully!

If you want to restore from a backup file other than
sageback.001, then you need to click on the **Setup** button
in order to select a different file (as shown in the following
illustration)

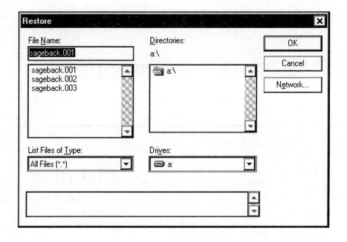

Select the file you want to restore and click **OK**.

Index

C

D

F

V

Notes

Notes

Notes